P9-EAJ-165

IMPROVEMENTS

your patio and deck

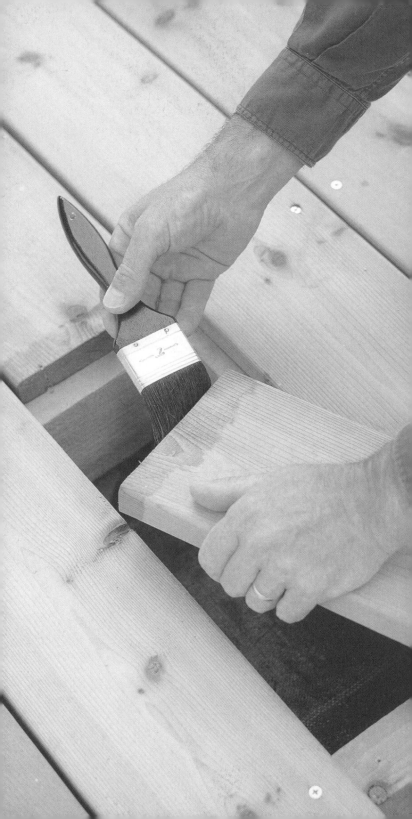

EASY HOME
IMPROVEMENTS

your patio and deck

STEWART WALTON

LEBHAR-FRIEDMAN BOOKS

New York • Chicago • Los Angeles • London • Paris • Tokyo

Lebhar-Friedman Books
425 Park Avenue
New York, NY 10022

First U.S. edition published 2000 by Lebhar-Friedman Books
Copyright © 2000 Marshall Editions Ltd., London U. K.

Published by Lebhar-Friedman Books
Lebhar-Friedman Books is a company of Lebhar-Friedman, Inc.

Originated in Singapore by Pica.
Printed and bound in China by Excel Printing.

Library of Congress Cataloging-In-Publication Data:
Walton, Stewart.
    Your patio and deck / Stewart Walton.--1st U.S. ed.
      p. cm.-- (Easy home improvements)
    ISBN 0-86730-793-5 (alk. paper)
    1. Patios--Design and construction--Amateurs' manuals. 2. Decks
(Architecture, Domestic)--Design and construction--Amateurs'
manuals. I. Title II. Series.

TH4970.W358 2000
690'.893--dc21   00-021308

Project Editor Ian Kearey
Designed by Paul Griffin
Photographer Alistair Hughes
Managing Editor Antonia Cunningham
Managing Art Editor Patrick Carpenter
Editorial Director Ellen Dupont
Art Director Dave Goodman
Editorial Coordinator Ros Highstead
Production Amanda Mackie
Indexer Jill Dormon

Front cover photography: **Ron Sutherland/ The Garden Picture Library**
Back cover: **Alistair Hughes**

Visit our Web site at lfbooks.com

Volume Discounts
This book makes a great gift and incentive. Call (212) 756-5240 for
information on volume discounts.

Note

contents

introduction

When you mention "home improvements" to people, the great majority tend to think purely in terms of the interior and structural fabric of a building. By doing this, they are ignoring the many opportunities for creativity and improvement in a yard or garden, whatever its size and condition. To give just one example, how often do we see a nicely tended lawn and flower borders marred by plastic chairs and tables? Away with them, and set about making stylish garden furniture from nature's own material—wood!

In this book, I designed the projects to be accessible to as wide a range of people as possible. In the introduction to each set of step-by step photographs and text, the project is given a skill rating of Beginners, Intermediate, or Advanced. Of course, to give just one example, someone with experience in woodworking, for whom cutting joints poses no problem, may find using a sewing machine a tough proposition, and the reverse will be true for a practiced tailor or seamstress.

The important thing is to look at all the stages of each project before you tackle it and, above all, take your time—the times given in the introductory section for the projects assume you have all the materials and tools to hand and can work uninterruptedly until you have finished. The additional work needed to finish a project—treating wood, applying protection, painting, and varnishing—are not included in the times, nor are drying times for glue, wood putty, and finishes.

For the larger-scale projects—building a patio from bricks or pavers, or building a wooden deck—I have included a rough guide to how long you can expect to take on the marking out and preparation; once this is done, the time will depend on the area to be covered and the actual materials you use.

Note that the dimensions given in the Materials lists are for the finished size of each component; you can adapt projects such as the water garden or planter to fit your own requirements. If you are planning to change the size radically, you may have to reconsider the width and depth you use for each component, both for strength and proportions.

When it comes to tools, the golden rule is that you get what you pay for. Inexpensive tools may seem a bargain, but their drawbacks can range from measuring inaccurately to falling apart while working—and for power tools, this can lead to injury or worse. Make a careful check on secondhand tools, and inspect the condition of the wiring in electrical tools.

Don't let these dire warnings put you off. If you follow the manufacturer's instructions, and wear protective clothing where necessary or prudent, you should not have a problem. Good tools do cost, so build up your tool kit as and when you can; and to save spending money on equipment that may only be used once or twice, most rental stores hire out large and small power tools by the day or weekend.

I hope you get enjoyment and a sense of having achieved something worthwhile out of these projects.

Stewart Walton

chapter 1
Planters

making a water garden

This mini water garden is ideal for a garden of any size. If your garbage can has handles, trim off the top of the can just below them. You can use a wider or taller container than the one shown here, but you'll need more wood. A smaller container will need less wood.

Materials (all lumber is softwood unless otherwise stated)

19½-in.-diameter round plastic garbage can • 30 in. sq. plywood (for template) • 16-in.-long wood strip (for template) • Screw (for template) • 16 pieces 1 x 2 x 15 in. • 8 pieces 1 x 6 x 14 in. • 4 pieces 1 x 2 x 4 in. • 24 pieces 1 x 3 x 24 in. • Brads • Wood glue • 1½-in. bright zinc-plated screws • 2½-in. bright zinc-plated screws • Exterior wood glue • Exterior wood putty • Exterior woodstain and/or varnish

Tools

Carpenter's pencil • Protractor • Combination square • Metal straightedge • Triangle with 45-degree angle • Hammer • Crosscut saw • Power drill with ⅛ in. twist, countersink, and screw bits • Putty knife • Coarse- and medium-grit abrasive paper • Sanding block

Skill level

Advanced

Time

8 hours

1. To make the template, drive a screw through one end of a 16-in.-long wood strip, and drill a hole to accept a pencil 10 in. away from the screw—or half the width of your container plus ½ in. With the screw of this tool centered on 30-in.-sq. plywood, draw a circle slightly larger than the diameter of your container.

2. Using a metal straightedge and triangle with a 45-degree angle, divide the circle into 16 equal sections by first making a cross to get four sections. Divide these sections in half with a second cross, then divide the eight sections. Draw a square around the circle, with the center of each side meeting the circle.

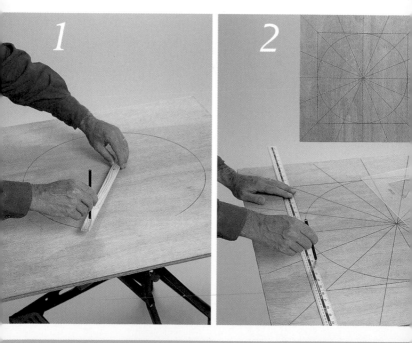

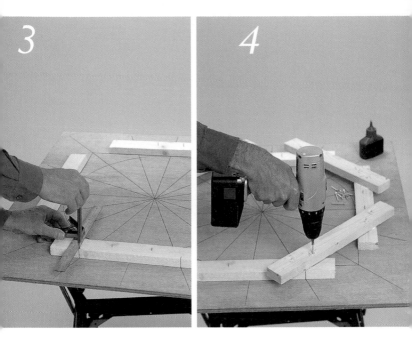

3 Secure four pieces of 15-in.-long 1 x 2 aligned against the outside edges of the square, using brads nailed down halfway. Near each end, mark where the pieces intercept the diagonal lines; mark the side edges and across the face of the work.

4 Attach four more pieces of 15-in.-long 1 x 2 to the work. Center each one at a corner between two attached pieces. Make new marks on the attached pieces to note their positions, and add glue between these marks. Reposition the pieces; at each end drill two pilot holes, countersink them, and drive in screws. Now remove the brads, using the claw end of your hammer.

5 Use a crosscut saw or jigsaw to trim the ends flush with the adjacent pieces. At each side of the octagonal, cut the end farthest from you, then the one closer to you. Repeat the procedure to make a second octagonal collar so that you have one for the top and one for the bottom of the container.

6 On your template, mark every line that dissects the circle, measuring in 1 in. from the circumference. Draw a line between each mark, forming an octagonal inside the circle. These marks will be used to measure the pieces that form the top, which will be used to cover the edges of the container.

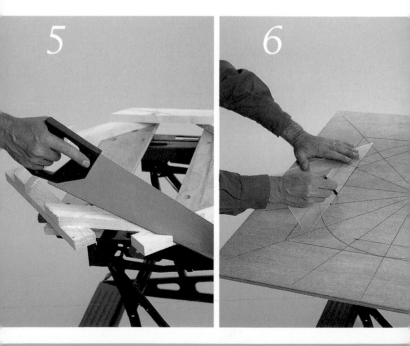

7 Use the template to mark cutting lines on the eight pieces of 14-in.-long 1 x 6 in. softwood, one at a time. Align the first piece on one side of the octagonal along the outside edge. On each end of the work, draw diagonal lines up the side edges and across the face. Cut along the marked lines, using a crosscut saw or jigsaw. Work around the template for each piece, stopping after the seventh piece.

8 To ensure a snug fit, with each cut piece in position on the template, position the last length of wood, and use the ends of the adjacent pieces to mark the lines on it. After cutting the work, position it in its place on the template, in preparation for the next step.

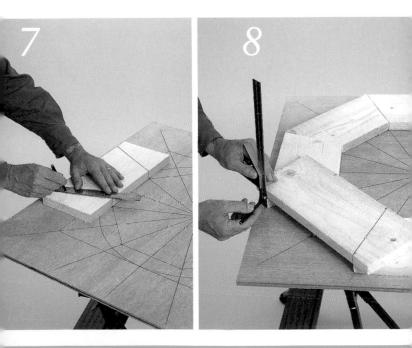

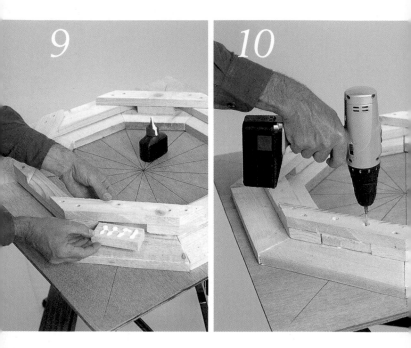

9 To mark the placement for the collar, lift one piece up at a time and use a combination square to transfer marks from the square on your template to the face of the pieces. Apply glue between the side edges of each piece, then repeat on the bottom surfaces of the collar that will rest on the "top." With the collar in position at the marks, apply glue to the top and bottom surfaces of four pieces of 4-in.-long 1 x 2 and insert them in the gaps between collar and top.

10 Screw down the collar, using 2½-in. screws at the raised sections and 1½-in. screws elsewhere. At the center of each section, drill a pair of pilot holes, countersink them, and drive in the screws.

11 Cut 24 pieces of 1 x 3 to length, using the height of your container plus ¼–½ in. clearance—the one shown here is 22 in. high. For a wider container, you may need additional lengths. For a smaller container, you can use 1 x 2s.

12 Attach four 1 x 3s to opposite ends of the top and collar, aligning them flush to a corner edge of the octagon. Apply glue to one end of a 1 x 3 and the surface that will be contacting the collar. With the work squared, drive in a pair of screws after drilling and countersinking the holes. Alternate between the top and bottom pieces of the collar, and make sure the screws go into the sides of the wood and not the end grain, which will cause splits.

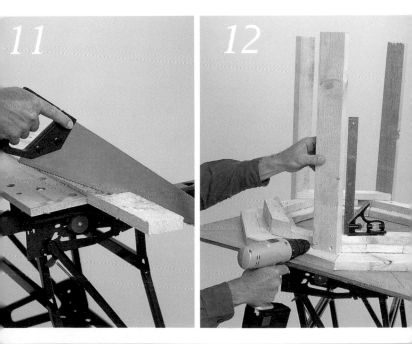

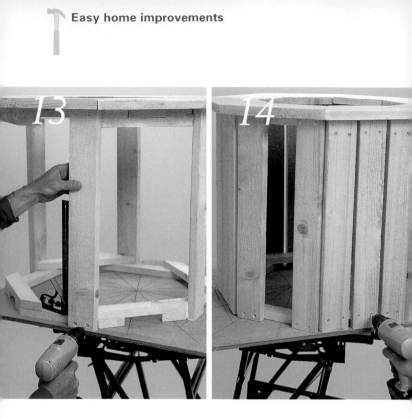

13 Remove the work from your surface and position the bottom collar on it. After applying glue to the free ends of the 1 x 3s already attached to the top collar, as in step 12, position them around the bottom collar and follow step 12 to attach them.

14 Continue attaching the 1 x 3s, first to the ends of each side of the octagonal. Then attach the remaining 1 x 3s, centering them between the side ones.

Helpful hints

The container, with its wooden surround, can be used to pot a tree, but first drill several drainage holes in the bottom. You can fill the bottom with styrofoam peanuts to assist drainage and make the container lighter for moving.

15 Where the screw heads will be visible, fill in the screw holes with wood putty. Use a putty knife or old woodworking chisel to push the filler into the holes. Also apply putty to fill any gaps in the joints of the top. Allow the filler to completely dry. Using coarse-grit abrasive paper, sand down the work to remove any splinters. Also use medium-grit abrasive paper to sand the top piece—it is more likely to come into contact with people.

16 To finish your water garden, place the garbage can in its final position, fill in the bottom quarter with pond compost. Add a layer of gravel on top of it to keep the compost from rising to the surface of the water. For smaller plants, build a ledge with a few bricks, and place the plant on it with the top of the pot about 2 in. below the water line.

making a
wooden planter

A good, solid planter allows you to experiment with combinations of potted plants out of doors. You can choose the finish you want, to blend in or contrast with the other features of the deck, patio, or yard.

Materials (all lumber is softwood unless otherwise stated)
3 pieces 1 x 4 x 40 in. • 2 pieces 1 x 2 x 12 in. • 4 pieces 1 x 3 x 4 in. • 4 pieces 1 x 3 x 6 in. • 2 pieces 1 x 3 x 40 in. • 2 pieces 1 x 3 x 15 in. • 14 pieces 1 x 2 x 38 in. • 10 pieces 1 x 2 x 13 in. • 4 pieces 1 x 2 x 9 in. •

⅛ x 24 x 48 in. plywood • 1¾-in. bright zinc-plated screws •
1½-in. brads • Exterior wood glue

Tools

Combination square • Tape measure • Carpenter's pencil
• Crosscut saw • Power drill with pilot hole, screw, and
½ in. bits • Hammer • Putty knife

Skill level

Intermediate

Time

4 hours

1 To make the base, clamp together three pieces of 1 x 4, standing on edge. Measure and mark them at 36 in. on the exposed edges and faces. Using a crosscut saw, cut them to length. Now clamp together two pieces of 1 x 2. Measure and mark them at 10 in., and cut them to length.

2 Set the three pieces of 1 x 4 together, edge to edge. Position the 1 x 2s across the 1 x 4s, one at each end; use a scrap piece of 1 x 2, on edge, to mark the spacing about 1 in. in from the edges. Apply glue along one surface of the 1 x 2s, and where they will contact the 1 x 4s. Center and drive screws through each 1 x 4—for hardwoods, first drill pilot holes.

3 Drill four ½-in. drainage holes in each 1 x 4, spaced evenly apart. Place scrap wood under the work where you are drilling to prevent the work from splitting and to protect your work surface.

4 Cut four pieces of 1 x 3 to 3 in. long and another four to 5 in. long. Make a miter cut in each one. Measure up ½ in. from a corner, then use a combination square to draw a 45-degree angle. Clamp the wood and cut it on the waste side of the line, using a crosscut saw.

Helpful hints

To save time and effort when cutting two or more pieces of lumber to identical lengths, clamp them together and cut them all at once.

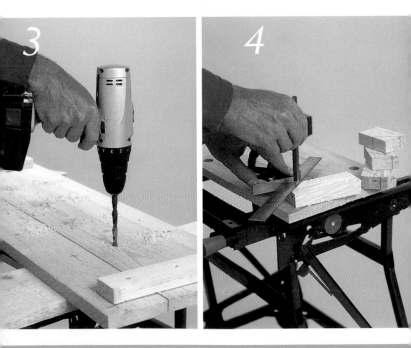

5 Assemble the mitered pieces to form the feet for the base. The longer ones will fit along the front and back edges; the shorter ones along the sides. For each foot, draw the position on top of the base to establish where to nail. Apply glue to all the contacting surfaces and position the pieces under the base; then nail in brads about 1 in. from each end, centered over the width of the piece.

6 For the top frame, cut two pieces of 1 x 3 to 36 in. and another two of the same dimensions to 13 in. To miter the ends, overlap the adjacent pieces and square them. Draw pencil marks along the sides on each piece of wood. Draw a diagonal between the lines, and use them to cut miters on the waste side of the lines. Mark the waste sides to check that you miter the corners in the correct directions.

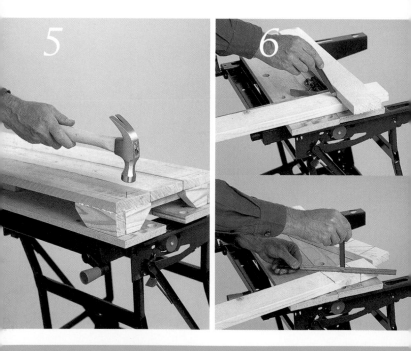

7 To make the planter box, measure, mark, and cut 14 pieces of 1 x 2 to 35 in., 10 pieces to 11 in., and 4 pieces to 7½ in., using the crosscut saw. Again, to save time and effort, you can clamp together up to four pieces to be cut to the same length.

8 Stain the pieces, following the instructions provided by the manufacturer. You can stain them different colors if you wish—here, the top and bottom frames were stained a darker color. Allow the stain to dry completely before you begin the assembly. You can prop the pieces on two lengths of scrap wood to prevent the stain from adhering to the work surface.

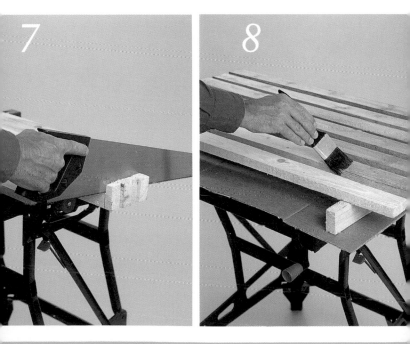

9   Cut the pieces for the bottom frame: two 1 x 2s cut to 35 in. and two cut to 7½ in. Do a test fit to get the pieces square and centered over the base before securing them in place with screws.

10   Attach the side pieces by alternating the long and short lengths. Apply glue to each corner of the facing surfaces. Position two long pieces, making sure they are square with the ends of the bottom frame, and secure them in place with brads. Apply glue to each corner and secure a pair of short side pieces; continue alternating between the long and short pieces, saving the two 7½-in. pieces for the top row.

11 Hold the plywood to the planter, with one edge in a corner, and mark where to cut it to length. Make the cut with the saw, saving the leftover plywood for the side piece. Insert the plywood, mark the height, and cut two pieces at 11½ x 31 in. and two at 11½ x 7 in. Apply glue to the edges, and use brads to secure the plywood inside the box to the top and bottom side pieces. Continue until all four sides are covered.

12 To secure the top frame to the box, apply glue to the contacting surfaces and secure the pieces in place with brads every 2 in. If the planter will be handled often, use screws every 4 in.—countersink the screw holes and apply filler over the screwheads (see page 19). Touch up the stain.

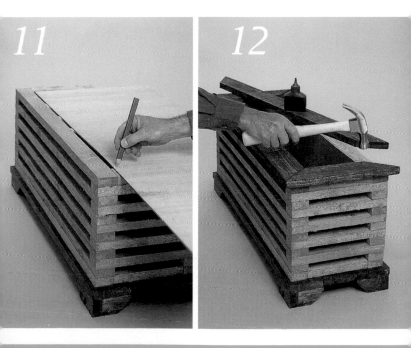

arranging a
hanging basket

Hanging baskets always look attractive above a patio or deck, and there are many designs of brackets available at garden centers and by mail order. Choose a mixture of plants, with some growing upward and others hanging or tumbling over the side of the basket.

Materials
Water-retaining granules • Soil-free potting mixture • Wire basket • Bucket or large flowerpot • Coco matting or other liner • Plastic plant-pot saucer • 8 ivy plants • 2 geraniums • 6 Petunias

Tools
Trowel

Skill level
Beginner

Time
20 minutes per basket

1 Prepare the potting mixture by adding water-retaining granules to a soil-free potting mixture—about 1¾ oz. of granules per 1⅓ gal. of potting mixture—and mix the two together thoroughly.

2 Stand the wire basket on a large flowerpot or bucket, and line the basket with coco matting or your preferred choice of liner. Loosen the matting by pulling it apart, or "teasing" it, as you line the basket. Place a plastic plant-pot saucer in the base of the basket, and half-fill the basket with the potting mix.

3 Plant four trailing ivy plants at this level, spaced evenly apart, pushing the roots through the matting and firming them into the potting mixture. Add more potting mixture, pressing it firmly into the sides of the basket, but leaving it light and loose within the center of the basket to allow for the rootball of the new plants. Plant another four ivy plants to trail between the lower four.

4 Loosen the soil around the roots of the main plants, then plant the two geraniums alongside each other in the center. Fill in all the gaps between the geraniums and the trailing ivy plants with petunias. You can use the trowel to push back the soil to make room for the new plants.

Outdoor furniture

making a
wooden bench

This strong, versatile bench is relatively easy to construct, and will last a long time if it is weatherproofed adequately. For a rustic look, you can leave the wood slightly rough-cut, but remove any splinters or protruding slivers of wood.

Materials (all lumber is softwood)

4 pieces 1 x 5 x 20 in. • 2 pieces 1 x 4 x 10 in. • 2 pieces 1 x 1 x 5 in. • 2 pieces 1 x 4 x 45 in. • 2 pieces 1 x 6 x 50 in. • Brads • 1¾-in. no. 8 bright zinc-plated screws • Exterior wood glue • Exterior-grade wood putty • Woodstain and/or varnish

Tools

Hammer • Combination square • Carpenter's pencil • Crosscut saw • Power drill with pilot hole, countersink, and screw bits • Putty knife • Coarse-grit and medium-grit abrasive paper • Sanding block • Brush

Skill level

Intermediate

Time

3–4 hours

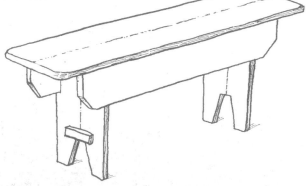

1 Place two 20 in. lengths of 1 x 6 together, making sure they are square, and nail them together with two brads about 4 in. from each end. These will eventually form the legs on one end of the bench. This way, it will take less effort to cut them, and they will be exact mirrors when they are assembled.

2 Measure 16½ in. from one end. Using a combination square, draw a line perpendicularly across the board. Rest the work on its edge and continue the line around the edge. Clamp the work in place and cut it with a crosscut saw along the waste side of the line.

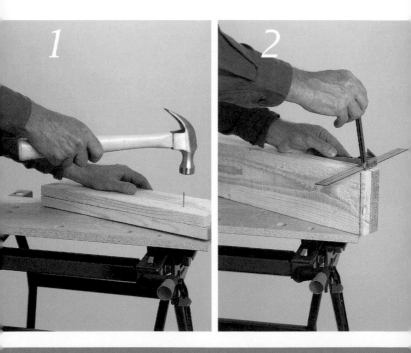

3 Measure 6 in. from the end of the board and make a perpendicular line 1½ in. long. At the end of the board, measure 2½ in. in from the corner, and draw a line to the end of the first line.

4 Securely clamp the work in place on its edge, with the marks at the top. Using a crosscut saw, cut down to where the two lines meet, cutting on the waste side. Reposition the work and cut down the second line to remove the wedge.

Helpful hints

Each of the two legs is made up from two pieces of wood. These are nailed together so you can cut them to form a precise mirror image.

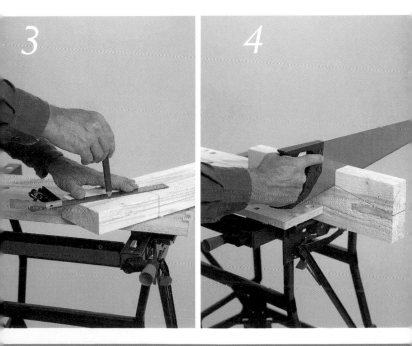

5 Hold the 1 x 4 for the side of the bench on its edge along the side of the work opposite the wedge cutout. From the corner diagonal to the wedge, draw a line alongside the 1 x 4 about 5 in. long. Lie the 1 x 4 down and turn it to align with the adjacent end of the work; draw a line until it meets the first line. Use a square to square off the lines along the edges. Cut out the notch.

6 Pry apart the pieces with an old chisel. Place them side by side, then lay a piece of 1 x 4 along the top edges with the notch for the joint. Mark the 1 x 4 at the notches and cut along the marks to about 8 in. long. Position the 1 x 4 and mark the positions for eight screw holes—four on each section, 1 in. in from the edges, and four 1 in. in from the center. Drill pilot holes.

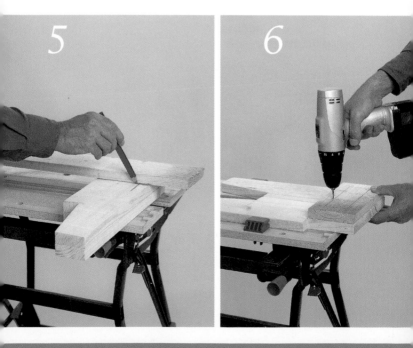

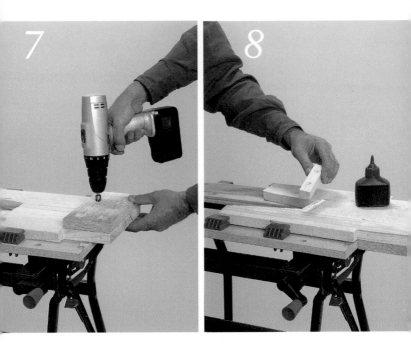

7 Countersink the holes so that the screw heads will be
flush with the wood. Apply glue along the edges of
the legs where they will meet, and to the surfaces
that will meet between the 1 x 4 support and the legs.
Set the 1 x 4 in place and screw the pieces together.
Wipe away any excess glue with a damp cloth.

8 Cut a piece of 1 x 1 to 4 in. long to support the bottom
of the legs. Drill two pilot holes about 1 in. from the
ends, and countersink them. Turn the legs over and
apply glue to the surface above the wedge and to the
1 x 1. Set the 1 x 1 in position and drive the screws in;
wipe away any squeezed-out glue. Repeat steps 1–8
to make the opposite legs.

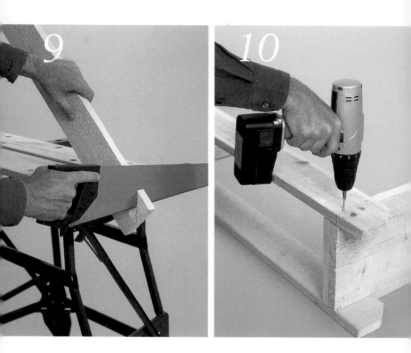

9   Cut a length of 1 x 4 to 41 in., and miter a corner at each end. Mark the center of the end and use the combination square to draw a 45-degree angle line to the edge. Clamp the work with the line vertical, and use the crosscut saw to cut along the line. Repeat at the opposite corner on the other end. Cut a second length in the same way.

10 Make a mark 3 in. from each end at the top edge (without the miters). To assemble, position one leg section with its outside edge at the 3 in. mark. Drill and countersink a pair of pilot holes 1 in. from the ends, centered over the main leg piece. Apply glue to the two surfaces, and drive in the screws. Continue assembling the legs and side pieces.

11 Cut two lengths of 1 x 6 to 46 in. Miter the corners as in step 9. Mark 5½ in. from the unmitered end. Position the board on the bench at these marks. Center pilot holes over the leg supports, 1½ in. from the outside edge, and 1 in. from the center. Mark screw holes along the edge 10½ in. in from these holes. Countersink the holes, apply glue to the two surfaces and along the side edge of the bench, and drive the screws in.

12 Cover the screw heads with wood putty. When it is dry, sand it flush to the surface. Sand the work to remove any splinters, starting with coarse-grit abrasive paper, then switching to medium-grit. Finish by applying a wood stain or varnish.

making a garden table

Designed to match the wooden bench, this timeless table uses dado joints in its construction.

Materials (all lumber is softwood)

4 pieces 1 x 6 x 30 in. • 2 pieces 1 x 2 x 12 in. • 2 pieces 1 x 5 x 24 in. • 2 pieces 1 x 5 x 40 in. • 2 pieces 1 x 4 x 24 in.• 2 pieces 1 x 6 x 40 in. • 4 pieces 1 x 5 x 50 in. • 1¾-in. bright zinc-plated countersunk screws • 1⅝-in. brads • Exterior wood putty • Exterior wood glue • Exterior wood varnish

Tools

Hammer • Combination square • Carpenter's pencil • Crosscut saw • Old screwdriver or chisel • Wood chisel • Wood or rubber mallet • Power drill with pilot hole, countersink, and screwhead bits • Putty knife • Coarse-grit and medium-grit abrasive paper

Skill level

Intermediate

Time

4–5 hours

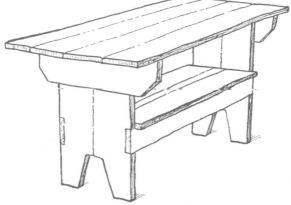

1. Nail together two 30-in. lengths of 1 x 6, using two brads at each end. Set the brads about 1½ in. from the edges of the wood and 4 in. from the ends. Make sure the edges of the wood are aligned so that they are squared.

2. With a combination square, measure and mark a line across the face of the wood about 2 in. from the end. Rotate the wood and continue the line over the edge.

Helpful hints

If you are new to woodworking, you will soon find out that a combination square will be one of the most useful measuring and marking tools and well worth the small investment.

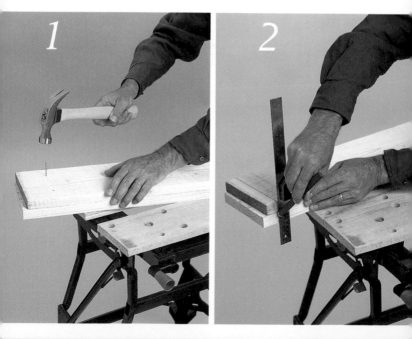

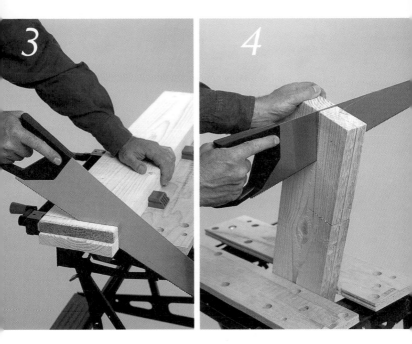

3 Cut the wood along the marked line, making sure you cut on the waste side. Measure 25½ in. from the cut, mark another line on the opposite end, and trim that end square (see page 44).

4 Decide which end is at the bottom, and then, from the bottom inside corner, measure along the length of the work 8 in. Draw a line perpendicular to the edge 2 in. long. From the same corner, measure 3 in. along the short edge, then draw an angled line to the end of the 2 in. line. Clamp the wood so the angled line is vertical for cutting, and cut along the lines on the waste side.

5 To make a notch, at the bottom outside corner measure up the length of wood 14 in. Support the piece of 1 x 4 that will be the shelf support, with its top edge at the mark, and draw guide marks on each side. Lay the work flat, then hold the edge of the 1 x 4 square to the work, and use it as a guide to draw the depth of the notch.

6 Saw down the sides of the notch on the waste side of the marks (the inside of the notch); then saw cuts to the depth line every ½ in. between the end cuts. Use an old wood chisel or screwdriver to pry apart the two pieces of wood; then knock out the brads with a hammer.

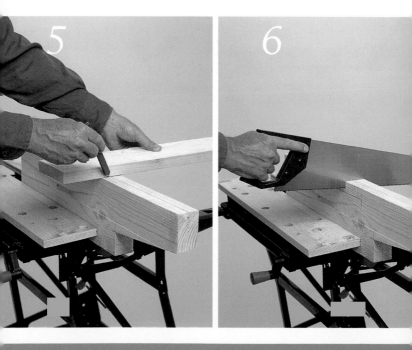

7 On each piece of wood, transfer the depth mark to the other side of the work. For a neat finish, score along the depth mark, using a utility knife and metal straightedge. Clamp the work in place on top of scrap wood. Using a mallet and wood chisel, bevel the face away from the waste, remove the waste wood in the notch. Start on one side, then turn the work over and remove the remaining wood. Pare the notch to smooth it, with the chisel's bevel face down.

8 Place the two pieces of the leg alongside each other. Set a piece of 1 x 2 at the top edge of the notches and mark along the notches onto the wood. Trim the wood. Mark positions for four screws 1 in. in from each side and spaced evenly apart. Drill pilot holes for the screws, going through the top piece of wood and one-third through the second piece.

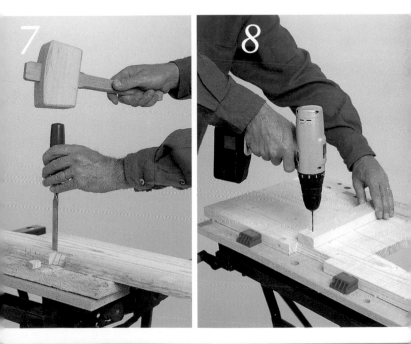

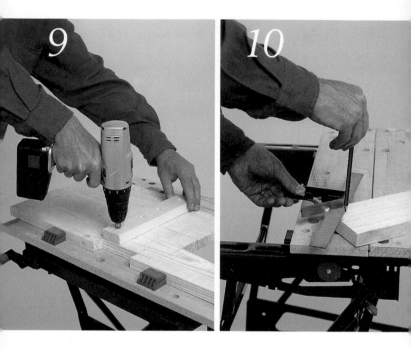

9 Use a countersink bit to make a recess for the screw heads. Apply glue to the edges of the leg pieces and between the cross support and the leg, then drive the screws in place. Wipe away any squeezed-out glue with a damp cloth. Repeat steps 1-8 to make the second "leg."

10 Cut two pieces of 1 x 5 to 20 in. On each piece of wood measure and mark the center at each end. Place the blade of a combination square set at a 45-degree angle at the center mark and draw a line along it. Use the line to make a miter cut, using a saw.

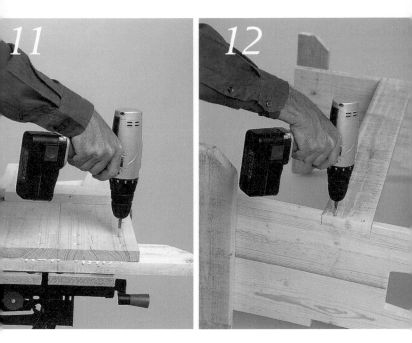

11 Center a table support at the top of a leg and drill two rows of pilot holes, four holes per row, spaced evenly apart and 1 in. in from the edges. (Use scrap 1 x 2 to keep the leg level.) Countersink the holes, apply glue to the surfaces of the leg and support, and drive the screws in place. Wipe away any squeezed-out glue. Repeat for the other leg and support.

12 Cut two pieces of 1 x 5 to 35 in. Assemble one length in a notch in each leg. At each end, drill a pair of pilot and countersink holes 1 in. from the edges. Apply the glue and drive the screws in place. Wipe away any excess glue. Repeat for the second piece of 1 x 5.

13 Cut a 1 x 2 and two 1 x 6s to 33 in. Before assembling, place the pieces across the lower supports to form a shelf. Trim to fit if necessary, then attach the 1 x 2 in the center, drilling a pilot hole and countersink at the center of each end. Secure a 1 x 6, drilling pilot holes and countersinks and adding glue, and repeat for the second piece.

14 Cut four 1 x 5s to 46 in. Draw perpendicular pencil lines 5 in. from each end. Place a board with one edge at the center of the table support. Drill a pair of pilot and countersink holes at each end, then apply glue, and drive the screws in place. Secure the end board, then repeat to secure the second inside and end boards.

Helpful hints

To save your fingers from damage when sanding—and to get the best results—make a rectangular sanding block from cork, foam, or wood that will fit your hand comfortably. Fold abrasive paper over so your hand can keep it in place.

15 Cover the screw heads with exterior-grade wood filler, using a putty knife. Allow it to dry, then sand down the table, using coarse-grit, then medium-grit abrasive paper to level the filler and smooth down edges that can produce splinters. Sand in the direction of the grain of the wood.

16 Apply exterior-grade wood stain and/or varnish, following the manufacturer's directions. Make sure you use the brush in the direction of the wood grain.

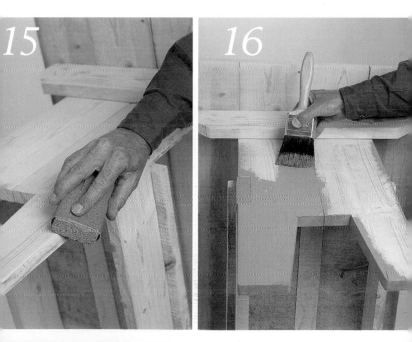

making a **storage box**

The weight of this patio box's lid will help deter smaller animals. If you live in an area with large animals, also attach a hasp to the front and secure the lid with a lock. Don't use the box for storing food or utensils for cooking.

Materials (all lumber is softwood unless otherwise stated)

4 pieces 1 x 2 x 35 in. • 4 pieces 1 x 2 x 24 in. • 1 piece ¾ x 22½ x 31½ in. marine plywood • 1 piece ¾ x 20½ x 31½ in. marine plywood • 30 pieces 3½ x 18 in. tongue-and-groove panel • 4 pieces 1½ x 2 x 24 in. • 1 piece 1½ x 2 x 32 in. • 4 pieces 1½ x 3 x 24 in. • 3 standard 2-hole hinges with ¾-in. screws • 2 pieces hardwood molding 72 in. long •

¾-in. veneer brads • 1½-in. brads • 36-in. chain • ¾-in. wire staples • 1¾-in. bright zinc-plated screws • 4 rubber bumpers • Exterior wood glue

Tools

Crosscut saw • Carpenter's pencil • Combination square • Power drill with ⅛ in., countersink, and screw bits • Hammer • Bradawl • Miter box and backsaw or miter frame

Skill level

Intermediate

Time

5–6 hours

1 To make a frame, cut two lengths of 1 x 2 to 31½ in. and two lengths to 20½ in. Join the pieces with butt joints, with the ends of the short lengths between the long ones. Rest the lengths on a flat surface, and use a combination square to mark the width of the short length on the top edge of the long one. Align the square at this mark, then place two screw marks ½ in. from the top and bottom and centered across the width of the butting piece.

2 Drill pilot holes for the screws at your pencil mark, then countersink the holes. Apply glue to the end of the short piece, position the two pieces, using a combination square to make sure they are square, and drive in the screws.

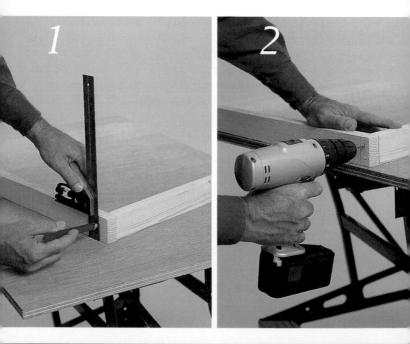

3 Continue forming the butt joints around the frame, making sure each time that the joints are square. When drilling, make sure the opposite end of the short length is secured in place with a clamp, or set it against a sturdy object. Repeat the procedure to form the second frame. Mark the bottom surface of the frames, which should be flush, with an X.

4 Set one of the frames on a flat surface, with the marked flush surface face up, and apply glue around the top edges. Set the smaller of the precut plywood pieces on top of the frame, with its edges flush with the frame. Using a length of 1 x 2 set on edge as a spacing guide, draw lines parallel to the sides of the plywood with a pencil.

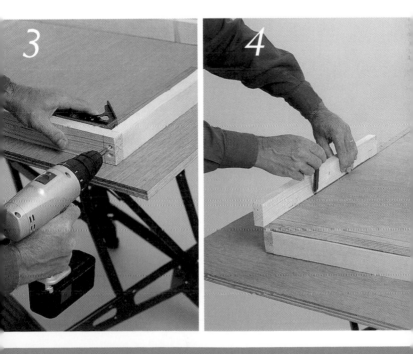

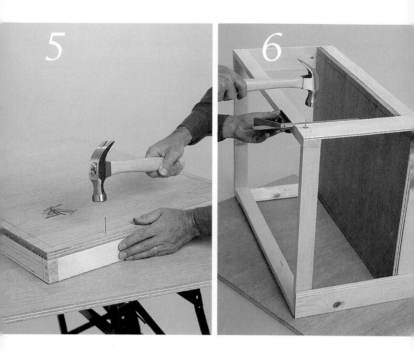

5 Center 1½-in.-long brads between the edges of the plywood and your guidelines. Hammer them in at the corners, just past the screws, then space brads apart every 3 in. Trim the tongue-and-groove panels to 15 in. long, using a crosscut saw.

6 Set the larger precut piece of plywood on the ground to create a level surface. Stand the frames on end about 15 in. apart, with the marked flush surface of the top frame facing away from the bottom frame and the plywood end of the bottom frame facing the top frame. At each corner, attach a piece of panel to the frames (see step 7). Stagger the panels so that there is no more than one piece on each side of the box, and make sure all the tongues are facing in the same direction.

7 To attach a panel, apply glue to the contacting surfaces and nail in a pair of 1-in.-long brads at each end. Use the combination square to keep the work square and the panel ends flush with the frames. As you continue to fill the side, insert the panels with the tongues fitting into the grooves, then nail them down.

8 When you reach the end of one side, you may need to trim a panel to fit. Use the adjacent corner panel as a guide to mark the panel to be trimmed, then cut it with a crosscut saw. If there is a small gap that will be covered with a leg, you don't have to fill it.

Helpful hints

If you have difficulty holding small nails or brads as you hammer them in, you can poke the point of the nail through a piece of thin cardboard, then hold the cardboard instead of the nail as you hammer it in place.

9 For the legs, cut four pieces of 1½ x 2 and four pieces of 1½ x 3 to 20 in. Apply glue on the contacting surfaces of a length of 1½ x 2 and along the corner of the front or back of the box. Drill and countersink a pilot hole 1 in. from the top and 2½ in. from the bottom. Drive in the screws. Attach the 1½ x 3 the same way, with screws centered on the 1½ x 2 at 2 in. from the top, 3 in. from the bottom, and one centered between.

10 To prevent fingers being crushed by the lid, attach rubber bumpers at each corner. Center them on the ends of the 1½ x 3 sections of the legs. To support the hinges, hold a length of 1½ x 2 along the back of the box along the legs. Mark their distance on the wood, then trim it with the saw.

11 To install the support, apply glue to the contacting surfaces and set the wood protruding from the top edge of the box the height of the bumpers. Make pencil marks for the hinges at the center and centered 6 in. from the ends. Drill pilot holes, countersink them, and drive in screws 2 in. from either side of the center marks for the hinges.

12 To attach a hinge, place one at its center mark—make sure it's facing the right way up—and use a bradawl to mark the screw holes. Drill out the bradawl marks to make pilot holes, then drive in the screws.

Helpful hints

To prevent the molding on the back edge from hitting the butt of the hinges, make hinge recesses with a chisel, or secure the molding protruding above the lid, and plane it level.

13 Rest the box on its back and raise it off the ground to the width of the lid, using scrap wood and cardboard. Draw a center line on the lid on the side near the box, and align this centered on the middle hinge, with the edge of the lid aligned with the butt of the hinges. Use the bradawl to mark the screw positions of the exterior screw for the two end hinges, drill pilot holes, and drive in the screws. Lift the lid up to check that it is square, then insert the remaining screws.

14 With the box upright, hold hardwood molding against the edge of one side—you can nail in a brad partway to hold it in place, but remove it after marking the wood. Draw a line up along the back side of the molding against the lid, then angle it out away from the lid to guide you when cutting it to form a miter. Using a miter box and backsaw or miter frame, saw a mitered end.

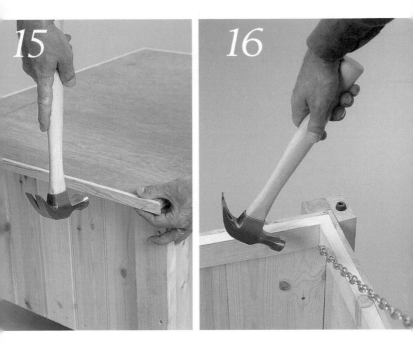

15 To secure the molding to the lid, apply glue to the two edges, then nail in veneer brads ½ in. from the ends and every 6 in. apart. To measure the next piece, turn the mitered end of the unused molding around to fit it snugly in the corner, then mark the uncut end. Make sure you miter the end of the second piece before measuring it. If the back strip is too wide, you may have to use a chisel to make recesses for the hinges, or set it above the hinges and plane it flush with the lid.

16 To fasten a chain to prevent the lid from flipping back, attach it with a wire staple at one end to the top frame inside the box and at the other end to the top inside corner of the lid.

making a
waterproof cushion

It's all very well making wooden benches and chairs for outdoor seating, but you need cushions when sitting for a while. Instead of bringing out interior cushions and running the risk of getting them dirty or wet, you can make matching exterior ones from easily cleaned vinyl. As you become more adept at using a sewing machine and the fabric, you'll bring down the time needed to make each cushion.

Materials
Vinyl material • Matching durable thread • Calico • Adhesive tape • Styrofoam peanuts

Tools
Tape measure • Scissors • Sewing machine • Curved sewing needle

Skill level
Intermediate

Time
1½ hours per cushion

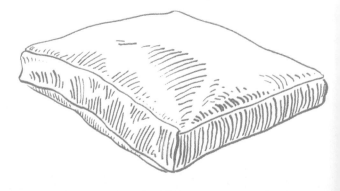

1 Measure the seat from back to front and side to side. Transfer these measurements, along with the depth that you want your cushion to be, to the back of your material, adding ⅝ in. all around for the seam allowance. To save on material, add the pattern for the sides of the cushion to the top edges of the top, back and to one side of the seat.

2 Carefully cut out the shapes along your measurement lines. Using a drinking glass as a template, draw a circle on the wrong side of the material at the center of the seat bottom. Cut out this circle.

Helpful hints

Vinyl is a thick, stiff material to work with at the best of times, so use the largest stitch setting available on your sewing machine to stop it from splitting.

3 Cut a square of calico 2 in. wider than the circle.
Center it over the hole and secure it to the back of the
vinyl with adhesive tape. Stitch the two pieces
together, using the widest stitch setting on your
sewing machine. Guide the edge of the circle along
the outside edge of the pressure foot. This will be
a drainage hole if the seat gets wet.

4 With the good sides of the material facing each other,
stitch together the side pieces, leaving ⅝ in. of the
material free at the top and bottom of the seam.
Double back at both ends of the seams to ensure
they don't pull free.

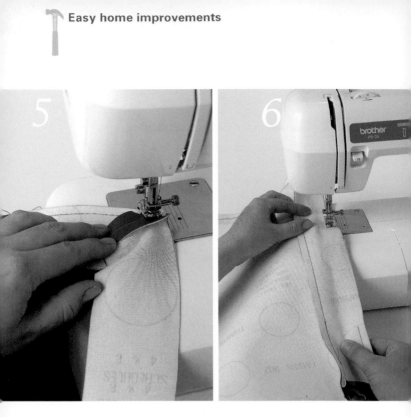

5 Attach the sides to the top with the right sides together, allowing a ⅝-in. seam. When you reach a corner, hold the flap at the seam on the side piece flat and stitch to the seam. With the needle completely lowered, raise the pressure foot and rotate the work. With the second flap from the side seam held flat, continue until you reach the start of this seam.

6 Sew the bottom piece to the sides with the right sides together, with a ⅝-in. seam, allowing a 6 in. gap. If the bottom material does not slide through the sewing machine, place a sheet of paper underneath it to help feed the material through.

7 Clip the seams at the corners without cutting into the stitches. Turn the material inside out through the gap, so the right side of the fabric is exposed. Push the material out at the corners from the inside.

8 Fill the cushion with styrofoam peanuts until it is firm and flat, but without bulging. The last stage is to sew the seam at the gap, using a back stitch. A curved needle will make the stitching easier; make each stitch about ¼ in. long.

Helpful hints

If you have not had much sewing experience, hold the pieces of fabric together with adhesive tape or paper clips. Just remove the tape or clips before the fabric reaches the needle.

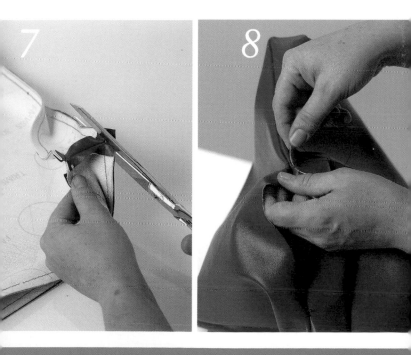

making a
plant stand

If space is limited in the patio—or even if it isn't—this plant stand is a stylish way to display your plants.

Materials (all lumber is softwood)

2 pieces 1 x 6 x 35 in. • 2 pieces 1½ x 1½ x 16 in. • 2 pieces 1½ x 1½ x 18 in. • 1 piece 1½ x 1½ x 30 in. • 1 piece 1 x 2 x 30 in. • 3 pieces 1 x 6 x 34 in. • Wood glue • 1¾-in. bright zinc-plated screws • Wood putty • Wood stain

Tools

Carpenter's pencil • Protractor • Triangle • Crosscut saw • Power drill with pilot, countersink, and screw bits • Putty knife

Skill level

Intermediate

Time

3–4 hours

1 To mark the steps on the side piece, use a protractor to find a 55-degree angle and draw a line about 4 in. long diagonally across the board. Use a triangle to draw a line at a 90-degree angle from the first line to the edge of the board—this line should be 5 in. long. From the second line, draw another line at a 90-degree angle 6 in. long, then a fourth line at a 90-degree angle 7¾ in. long; repeat the last two measurements, then draw one last line at a 90-degree angle.

2 On the last line, measure down 2 in. and draw a line at a 90-degree angle. From the inside angle on this bottom step, measure 2¾ in. and draw a line at a 90-degree angle 1 in. long. From the end of this line, draw another line to the point of the outside corner. Repeat as for the last step.

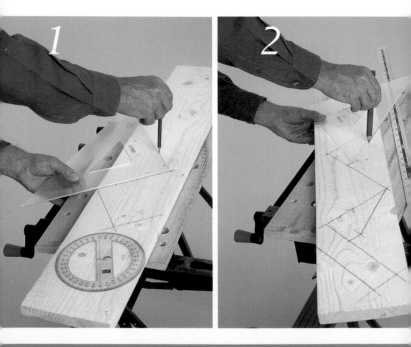

3 Clamp the work, and use a crosscut saw or jigsaw to cut along the exterior lines. Use this piece as a template to mark the second side piece, and cut that.

4 To make the support pieces, measure and mark two pieces of 1½ x 1½ to 14 in. long, two to 17 in. long, one to 26 in. long, and one 1 x 2 to 26 in. long. For the best results, make sure one end is square before measuring from it and cutting the second end.

Helpful hints

If you have a jigsaw, this is the best tool to use for cutting the angles on the side "stepped" pieces. As with all power tools, make sure you set it up properly before starting to cut , and wear protective gear.

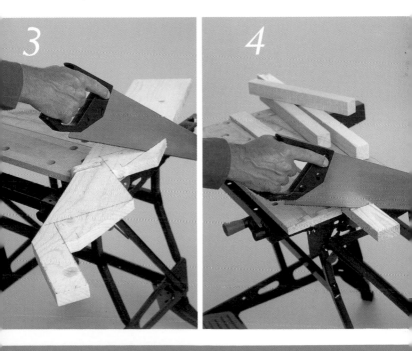

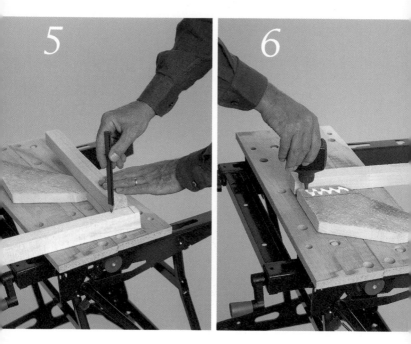

To assemble one side of the stand, hold a 17-in. length of 1½ x 1½ with its edge flush with the top edge of the bottom step. Hold a 14-in. length of 1½ x 1½ with its bottom edge flush with the bottom of the side piece and mark the width of the 17-in. length on it. Mark the back side.

Hold the unmarked end of the 1½ x 1½ length with its edges flush with the top corner of the side piece, and draw a line down its side. Apply glue in a zigzag pattern within the marked area. Screw the two pieces together (see step 8), using only one screw about 1 in. from the end.

7 Position the 17-in. length of 1½ x 1½ with one end aligned with the marks on the 14-in. length and the edge of the other end flush with the top edge of the bottom step. Use a combination square to make sure the two 1½ x 1½s are square, and mark the end and edge of the 17-in. length of the side piece.

8 Apply glue to the marked area, and then the end of the 17-in. length that will butt to the 14-in. length. Screw the 17-in. length in place, making sure the two 1½ x 1½s are still square. Before driving in a screw, drill a pilot hole and, if you are using a hardwood, drill a guide hole and countersink it. Add a second screw to the 14-in. length.

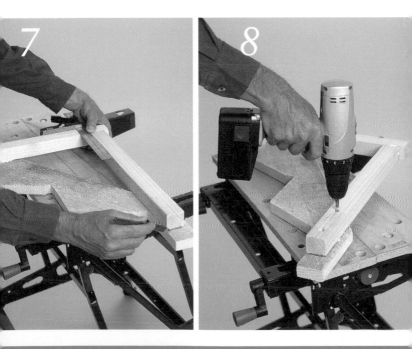

9 Where the two 1½ x 1½s meet, drill a pilot hole centered between the two pencil marks. Countersink and drive in a screw. Assemble the second side pieces.

10 Stand the two side pieces with their front edge up. Add glue to one end of the 26-in. length of 1½ x 1½ and to the exposed end of the wood already joined to the side piece. Place the 26-in. length in position, drill a pilot hole, countersink it, and drive in a screw. Repeat for the other side.

Helpful hints

Accurate measuring, marking, and cutting can be spoiled by screws that are inserted at the wrong angle, sometimes protruding through the wood. To avoid this, practice drilling straight, precise holes on scrap lumber.

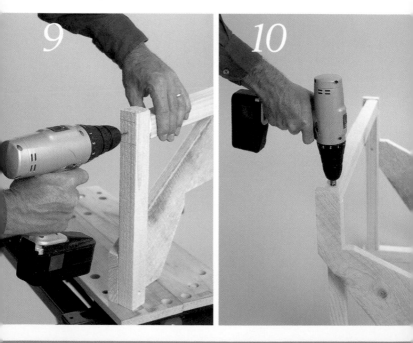

11 Apply glue to the surface of the 1½ x 1½s where they will meet the 1 x 2. Position the 1 x 2 with its ends flush to the side supports. At each end drill in a pilot hole, countersink it, and drive in a screw.

12 Cut three lengths of 1 x 6 to 30 in. With the stand the right way up, install the shelves, starting at the top and working your way down. For each shelf, apply glue to the side supports, center the shelf on the stand, and drill a pair of pilot holes centered over the side support on each end of the shelf. Countersink the pilot holes and drive in the screws. Finish off by covering the screw heads with wood filler, sanding the work down, and applying a stain and/or varnish.

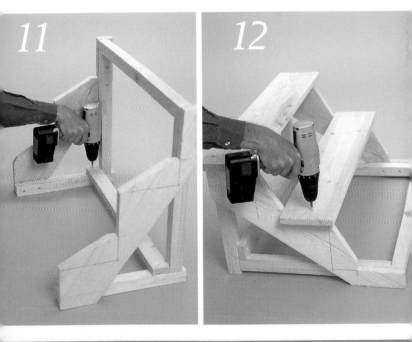

chapter 3
Patios and decks

making a
brick patio

Using bricks to make a patio, or extend an existing one, allows you to think creatively about the patterns you can make with the bricks. In addition, it pays to do some research into the different brick colors and textures available, because a contrasting patio can look good.

Materials

Bricks • Sharp sand • Pressure-treated lengths of 1 x 6 in.
• 1 x 2 x 12 in. pressure-treated wedges • 1½-in. screws •
Cement

Tools

Club hammer • Carpenter's pencil • Shovel • Carpenter's level • Power drill with screw bit • 3, 4, 5 triangle • Thick piece of wood • Rake • Rubber mallet • Broom • Water can

Skill level

Advanced

Time

Minimum 8 hours

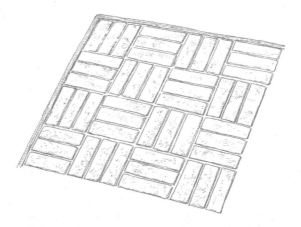

1 Lay a length of 1 x 6 for one side in position, using a 3, 4, 5 triangle (see page 86) to square it to the house. Pour a line of sand along its edge, and use this as a guide to dig a trench. Set the wood in the trench snugly against the edge toward the patio and level it. Tap in a stake flush to the top of the 1 x 2 at the end furthest from the house. Make a mark from the top equal to ⅛ in. for every 12 in. of patio. Tap down the 1 x 2 at this end to the mark on the stake.

2 Use the triangle to square the next length of 1 x 6 to the first, parallel to the house and level. Position the next 1 x 6 like the first, with the end farthest from the house, slightly sloping down. The last length should be level and parallel to the house.

3 To support the 1 x 6s, drive wedges down alongside
them at the ends and every 24 in. The top of the
wedges should be about 1 in. below the top of the
1 x 6. Secure the wedge to the wood with a screw.

4 Backfill the trenches with soil, making sure it covers
the top of the wedges. Tamp the soil down with a
thick piece of wood.

Helpful hints

*However well you lay the bricks, if the surface is not
prepared accurately, the finished patio will not look good.
To save on labor, consider hiring a professional to level the
site for the patio.*

5 Spread sand about 2 in. deep inside the area bordered by the 1 x 6s. Use a rake to spread it about, then tamp it down with a piece of plywood attached perpendicular to a board, or by stamping on it. Use the back of the rake to smooth the sand.

6 Stretch a length of string parallel to the house at the end farthest from it. Work along the first pair of marks (see Helpful Hints, opposite page) on the 1 x 6s. Attach each end of string to a stake, knitting needle, or tent peg, and drive them into the ground to hold the string taut. Start setting out the first course of bricks. Here, we used a traditional basketweave pattern, with three bricks in one direction alternating with three bricks in the other one; space them apart so they are set the length of a brick.

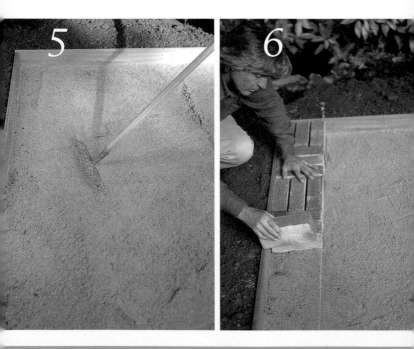

7 Move the string along for each row, and use a carpenter's level to make sure the bricks are flush. If a brick is set too high, use a rubber mallet to tap it down; too low, push extra sand under it with a trowel.

8 Make a cement-and-sand mixture of 4 parts sand to 1 part cement. Brush it over the bricks, pushing it into the cracks. Brush away the excess and sprinkle some water into the cracks. Repeat this procedure, brushing another batch of mixture over the bricks and watering it down.

Helpful hints

To avoid cutting bricks, make the size of the patio dividable by the bricks' length. Add 2 in. to the dimensions for the 1 x 6s. Draw a mark on the 1 x 6s 1 in. from the ends and each 9 in. in between.

building a
patio with pavers

As with the brick patio, the essential starting point for this project is that the ground is level—time spent getting the early part of the procedure right will save a lot of frustration and adjusting. Before buying the pavers, look around at what is available and choose a color and texture that will harmonize with the existing surroundings.

Materials

Concrete square pavers • Concrete edging pavers • Sharp sand • Cement • Water

Tools

3, 4, 5 triangle • Wood stakes • Club hammer • String • Carpenter's level • Shovel • Thick piece of lumber • Rake • Broom • Water can

Skill level

Advanced

Time

Minimum 8 hours

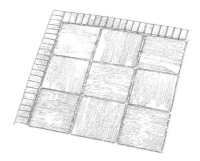

1 Start by marking where to dig a trench for the edging. Measure the area for your patio, then measure 4 in. inside from each corner to allow the same distance of backfill for the edging. Place a stake inside each of these corners and drive it in, using a club hammer. Tie string to the stakes.

2 Pour a line of sand along the string to mark where you will be digging. Pour the sand directly on top of the string. Remove the string.

Helpful hints

To make a 3, 4, 5 triangle for squaring corners, measure 36 in. on one length of 1 x 2, and 48 in. on a second length. Attach a third piece at these marks—it should measure 60 in. between them.

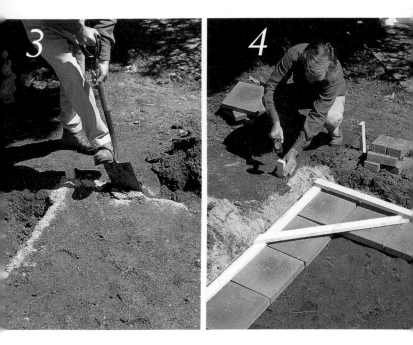

3 Dig a trench 4-in. wide along the line of the sand for the edging. It should be the depth of the length of the edging paving minus 2 in. Use the shovel to cut along the sand line. As you get to a corner, remove the stake. Fill the bottom of the trench with about 1 in. of sharp sand.

4 Lay a dry run of pavers along the edges of the patio, using the 3, 4, 5 triangle at the corners to keep the rows square. Along each side, run a length of string aligned with the edges of the pavers. To establish the height of the edging bricks, drive in two stakes on each side with a club hammer, and run lengths of string 2 in. above the top of the pavers. After the four strings are up, remove the pavers.

5   To create a slope away from the house, set a length of
    wood on top of a stake near the house, and on the
    stake at the far end of the string at the other end of
    the house. Place a carpenter's level on it and drive
    down the stake until they are level. For every foot of
    patio, lower the string ⅛ in. For example, for a 48-in.
    wide patio, lower the string ½ in.

6   Starting at a corner, set the edging pavers in place,
    standing them on end. Keep them aligned along the
    outside of the string, with the top edges just hitting
    the string.

7 Backfill the soil along the outside of the edging, then fill in the trench on the inside with sand. Use a thick length of lumber to tamp down, or compress, the soil and sand.

8 Fill in the area of the patio between the edging with a 2-in. layer of sand. Spread it out with a rake, then tamp it down firmly by walking over it; finally, smooth the sand with the back of the rake.

Helpful hints

The first placement of the strings is for digging the trench for the edging, not for the pavers. To calculate pavers, subtract 4 in. from each end of the trench.

9 Position a string line, and stakes running parallel with the line, at the end of the patio farthest away from the house. This new line should be set the width of your paver inside the first line. Set the first row of pavers between the sand line and the new line, using a carpenter's level to keep them flush with each other and the top of the edging.

10 Move the string for each new row of pavers. As you continue positioning the pavers, use a rubber mallet to tap a paver that sits too high, or use a trowel to push some extra sand under a paver that is set too low. Continue until all the pavers are in place.

11 Mix a sand-and-cement mixture, using 4 parts sand to 1 part of cement. Brush this over the patio, pushing it so that it fills the cracks, then brush off any excess on the face of the pavers.

12 To help compress the mixture, sprinkle some water into the cracks—however, don't put in so much that the mixture splashes out. Spread the sand-and-cement mixture over the patio again, and add a little more water as required.

Helpful hints

The area covered by the pavers does not have to butt up to the house—you can position it about 24 in. away from the house and fill the gap with gravel, pebbles, or perhaps a flower border.

building a
deck

In any yard or garden, a wooden deck can be the place where you can eat, relax, or display a wide variety of plants. Before you start construction, the site where you build the deck should be cleared and level—this is hard manual labor, and you may wish to hire someone to do this while you plan the finished look.

Materials

4 x 4 in. Southern yellow pine or pressure-treated lumber, 24 in. per post • String • Bricks or preformed concrete feet • 2 x 4 in. pressure-treated pine or other lumber • 1 x 4 in. pressure-treated lumber • 18-in. carriage bolts • Cement • Sand • Aggregate • Ground cover • Joist hangers • 1½-in. galvanized nails • Creosote • 2½-in. stainless steel decking screws

Tools

Combination square • Tape measure • Carpenter's pencil • Crosscut saw • Power drill with pilot hole, countersink, and ½-in. screw bits

Skill level

Advanced

Time

Minimum 8 hours

1 Mark the area where you plan to lay your deck, using
   string tied around wedges driven in at the corners; use
   a 3, 4, 5 square to make sure the corners are squared
   (see page 86). To support the deck, you'll need posts
   every 48 in. apart in rows running parallel to the house,
   with the rows 24 in. apart. For each post, dig a hole
   18 in. deep, making sure the bottom is flat. Set a brick
   or concrete foot in the bottom.

2 Along each row of posts parallel to your house,
   position a length of 2 x 4 at each side of the posts to
   form beams. Clamp the 2 x 4s to the corner posts
   about 1 in. above the ground. Use a carpenter's level
   vertically on the posts and horizontally on the 2 x 4s
   to ensure they are level, then adjust and reclamp
   as required.

3 Drill in a pair of holes through the 2 x 4s and posts; as you drill, pull the bit back to help remove the sawdust from the hole. Insert a pair of carriage bolts and tighten the nuts with a socket wrench. After one bolt has been inserted, you can remove one of the clamps for easier access.

4 Mix together 1 part cement to 4 parts sand and 4 parts aggregate; add a little water to just moisten it. Fill the post holes with this mixture. As you fill the hole, tamp it down with a length of 2 x 4 to compress the mixture and remove any air bubbles. After the final tamping, you can finish the surface with the trowel.

5   Trim the top end of the posts flush with the top edge of the beams, using a crosscut saw with the blade at their level. Keep your free hand away from the work—the saw may jump forward as you finish the cut. If you are using pressure-treated wood, protect the cut ends from rot and insects by painting them with creosote.

6   To prevent tall weeds from growing through the deck, cover the soil with a plastic ground cover that will block out light. Lay the plastic between the rows of beams and trim it at the end with a utility knife. Cover the ends with some soil to hold it down. Don't worry if the ends do not overlap—this will allow rain water to dissipate into the ground instead of forming puddles.

7 Cut 2 x 4 joists to fit between the rows of beams. To accurately mark the size, set each joist in its final position. Cut it with a saw, then nail a pair of joist hangers to each end of the beam.

8 Nail the joists to the beams, placing them centered 18 in. apart and using 1½-in. galvanized nails. Make sure the top edge of the joist is flush with the beams. Continue securing them between all the rows.

Helpful hints

The maximum length available for lumber is 16 ft. If you can keep the dimensions of the deck within this measurement, you won't have to worry about creating seams across the deck as you lay the planks.

9 With your frame now almost complete, use a
straightedge to mark the ends of the beams, then trim
them with a crosscut saw. Coat all the cut surfaces
with creosote as in step 5 if you are using wood that
has been pressure-treated.

10 Position the first plank at the end farthest from the
house and running parallel to it, protruding 1 in.
beyond the frame. Secure it with the decking screws.
Drill two rows of pilot holes for the screws and space
them 18 in. apart, centered into the frame. The screws
on the other planks will be screwed into the joists.

11 Lay down several planks at a time, placing ¼-in. spacers between them. Draw a line along the front, centered over the end joist. Use this line as a guide for driving in the screws. Once all the planks are secured, trim the ends of the planks to the shortest one by drawing a pencil mark along a straightedge and cutting with a saw.

12 For a neat finish, cover the ends of the planks with a skirt, a length of 1 x 4 set on end and positioned flush to the planks. Drive the screws into the end of the beams. Alternatively, you can create a shaped edge by using planks longer than your frame and trimming them; for example, in a curve or wave. If you're using pressure-treated wood, coat the cut ends with creosote, as in step 5.

chapter **4**

Repairs and treatments

repairing a **deck**

There comes a time in the lifespan of any deck when it shows signs of wear and tear, or it may suffer damage before that point. Either way, you have to do something about it, preferably before the area that needs to be replaced gets any larger.

Materials

Replacement lumber • Wood preservative • Screws

Tools

Power drill with countersink and screw bits • Combination square • Carpenter's pencil • Crosscut saw • Brush • Paint bucket

Skill level

Intermediate

Time

30 minutes

1 To replace a damaged section of decking, remove the whole length of affected board by unscrewing it. With the board aligned alongside its original position, find the joists that are closest to either end of the damage. Use a combination square and pencil to draw a line along the board where it would fall at the center of the joists—use the screw holes as a guide.

2 Use a crosscut saw to cut away the damaged wood, cutting on the waste side—the side where there is damaged wood.

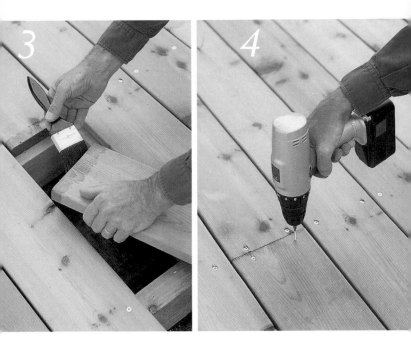

3 Treat the cut ends of the board with a wood
preservative or, if the wood has been pressure-treated,
with creosote. See pages 104–112 for information on
treating exterior lumber.

4 Position the sections with the butting ends meeting in
the center of the joists. On each end, drill a pair of
pilot holes, then countersink and drive in the screws
through the board and the jpist.

Helpful hints

*If a board has been stained or received other surface
damage, as long as it has squared ends, you can simply
unscrew it, turn it over, and screw it back down.*

treating wood for **outdoor use**

Even the toughest hardwood needs some degree of preserving and protecting from the ravages of the weather, and the same is more essential for softwood. Each of the methods shown here is easy—the secret of success lies in adequate preparation and meticulous working, making sure every part of the wood is treated or covered.

Materials

FOR PREPARING WOOD
Wood putty • Shellac

FOR TREATING PRESSURE-TREATED WOOD
Creosote

FOR PAINTING WOOD
Primer • Exterior-grade paint • Mineral spirit

FOR PRESERVING WOOD
Woodstain • Wood preservative stain

Tools

FOR PREPARING WOOD
Putty knife • Medium- or coarse-grit abrasive paper
• Sanding block • Brush

FOR TREATING PRESSURE-
TREATED WOOD
Bucket

FOR PAINTING OR
PRESERVING WOOD
Brush • Paint bucket

Skill level
Beginner

Filling and splinters

Cover screw heads, nail heads, and other small holes or cracks by pressing wood putty into the recesses, using a putty knife and leaving the putty protruding. Once the putty has dried, sand it smooth with abrasive paper.

To remove splinters, use abrasive paper wrapped around a cork, foam, or wood sanding block. Don't worry about smoothing down rough areas. These projects are made with coarse-sawn wood to give a rustic appearance.

Sealing knots

To prevent resin from seeping out of any knots in your wood, brush an acrylic sealer or shellac over them and allow to dry before the next stage. Check that a knot sealer matches the uses or woods that you intend to use.

Pressure-treated wood

If you have to cut this wood, the cut ends will need to be dipped in a bucket of creosote. Some brands of creosote are made to be brushed onto the ends— follow the instructions and wear protective gloves when brushing.

Natural finishes

To protect the wood while allowing its natural wood grain and color to show through, brush on a coat of wood preservative. Again, wear protective gloves and clothing if recommended.

You can add color to your wood and still allow its grain to show through by using a wood preservative that comes ready-mixed with an added color stain.

Paint finishes

Cover the wood with a primer—this will prevent the paint from seeping into the wood. Brush the paint, following the grain of the wood. Allow the primer to dry complotoly.

Next, brush on the paint. Cover any edges before painting the surfaces. Make sure you brush out any drips that accumulate in corners and under horizontal elements. You may need to apply a second coat of paint after tho first one dries.

glossary

Batten – a narrow strip of wood; often used to describe such a strip used as a support for other pieces

Bevel – any angle other than a right angle at which two surfaces meet

Butt joint – a simple joint where two pieces of wood meet with no interlocking parts cut in them

Countersink – to cut, usually drill, a hole that allows the head of a screw, nail, or brad to lie below the surface

Crosscutting – sawing wood across the grain

Dado – a shallow, wide groove cut across the grain of a piece of wood; a dado joint is one where a piece of wood is fitted into a dado

Galvanized – screw or nails covered with a protective layer of zinc; used mainly for exterior work

Hardwood – wood cut from trees, like oak, cherry, and elm, belonging to the botanical group *Angiospermae*

MDF – medium-density fiberboard; a prefabricated material that can be worked like wood

Miter – a joint made by cutting equal angles, usually at 45 degrees to form a right angle in two pieces of wood; cutting such a joint

Pilot hole – a small-diameter hole drilled into wood to act as a guide for the thread of a screw when driven in

Rabbet – a stepped recess cut along the edge of a piece of wood as part of a joint

Ripping – sawing wood along the grain

Sanding block – a cork or plastic rectangular block around which abrasive paper is wrapped

Softwood – wood cut from trees, like pine, maple, and cedar, belonging to the botanical group *Gymnospermae*

Template – a cut-out pattern on paper or cardboard, used to help shape wood

index

acknowledgments

All photographs taken by Alistair Hughes, except for:

8/9 Clive Nichols/ The Nichols Gdn, Reading; 32/33 Ron Sutherland/ The Garden Picture Library; 76/77 Michael Paul/ The Garden Picture Library; 100/101 Clive Nichols/ The Nichols Gdn, Reading.

Illustrations by Stewart Walton.